Instructions For When I'm Gone

Valuable Info for Those You Leave Behind

CHRIS FAIRWEATHER

Note: This document is not designed to take the place of a will.

Published by Berhampore Press
Wellington, New Zealand.
All rights reserved
Copyright 2018
BerhamporePress@gmail.com

ISBN-13:
978-1986599856

ISBN-10:
198659985X

Table of Contents

Instructions 1

First Things First 3
    Who has possession of your last will and testament? 3
    Funeral/Life Insurance Cover Provider (if any): 3

Biographical Information 5
    Personal Information 5

Eulogy Help – Highlights of My Life 7
    Early life, schools attended, achievements, marriages etc. 7

Medical Information 9
    Doctor's name 9
    Medications I'm on 9
    Your views on life support 9

Caring for Children and Others Who Depend on Me 11

Care of My Pets 13

Business Interests 15

Property Holdings 17

Insurance Details (house, car, life) 19

Bank Account Details 21

Term Deposits & Bonds 23

Other Investments and Shares 25

Pension Plans & Annuities 27

Credit/Debit Card Information 29

Debts / Mortgages / Loans 31

Tax and Social Security Information	33
Tax Number's:	33
Social Security Number:	33
Other Important Information:	33
Vehicle Details	35
Donations to Make on My Behalf	37
Items of Value & Who Gets What	39
Clubs, Memberships, and Organizations	45
Power, Gas, Phone, and Other Service Providers	47
Email and Social Media Details	49
Do you want Facebook deleted?	49
Other notes re: Social Media:	49
After My Death	51
Organ donation?	51
Burial or Cremation?	51
Type of Funeral?	51
Please Invite the Following People to My Funeral	53
Final Letter to My Family	59
Special Instructions for My Service	61
Special Message to Mourners	63
Last Wishes	65
Words of Wisdom for My Friends and Family	67
Additional Information for Friends and Family	69

Instructions

This easy-to-complete book is an excellent place to gather useful information your friends and family will need once you've gone.

It provides a place to list information such as bank account numbers, insurance details, regular payments, personal information for funeral planning, and much more.

Make life easier for those you leave behind. They will certainly appreciate it — especially, as in their grief at your passing, they may overlook important things you'd like them to do.

Important Note: This book is not designed to take the place of a will. If you don't already have a *last will and testament* we suggest you get one drawn up as soon as possible. This book is designed to give additional information and clarity to those you leave behind. Having a will is the most important thing you can do to help loved ones left behind, this book comes a close second.

First Things First

Who has possession of your last will and testament?

Name:_____

Address:_____

Phone:_____ Email:_____

Name of executor of will:_____

Address: _____

Phone:_____ Email:_____

Name of power of attorney: _____

Address: _____

Phone:_____ Email:_____

Funeral/Life Insurance Cover Provider (if any):

Name of Company: _____

Address: _____

Phone: _____ Email_____

Biographical Information

Personal Information

Date of birth:

Place of birth:

Mother's name:

Father's name:

Sibling's name/s:

Other significant relatives:

Eulogy Help – Highlights of My Life

Early life, schools attended, achievements, marriages etc.

8

Medical Information

(Handy in case you become infirm)

Doctor's Name:_____

Contact Details: _____

Specialist Name: _____

Contact Details:_____

Medications I'm on:
1.
2.
3.
4.
5.
6
7.
8.
9.
10.

Your views on life support:

Caring for Children and Others Who Depend on Me

NAME	INSTRUCTIONS

Care of My Pets

PET'S NAME	INSTRUCTIONS

Business Interests

BUSINESS	SHARE	ESTIMATED VALUE

Property Holdings

PROPERTY DETAILS	INCOME	VALUE

IF RENTING LIST LANDLORD	CONTACT DETAILS	
WHERE IS YOUR LEASE KEPT?		

Insurance Details (house, car, life)

COMPANY	ITEM INSURED	POLICY NUMBER

Bank Account Details

BANK	BRANCH	ACCOUNT NUMBER

Note any automatic payments that will need closing here:

Do not put bank account passwords in this book

Term Deposits & Bonds

DEPOSIT OR BOND	DETAILS	VALUE

Other Investments and Shares

INVESTMENT	DETAILS	ESTIMATED VALUE

Pension Plans & Annuities

SOURCE	DETAILS	MONTHLY INCOME

Credit/Debit Card Information

BANK & BRANCH	CARD TYPE	CARD NUMBER

30

Debts / Mortgages / Loans

NAME	DETAILS	I OWE	THEY OWE
	You can use more than one line if necessary.		

Tax and Social Security Information

Tax Number's:

1. State:

2. Federal:

Social Security Number:

Who Normally Does Your Tax?

Name:_____

Address:_____

Phone:_____Email:_____

Other Tax Information:

Vehicle Details

VEHICLE	PLATE NUMBER	INSTRUCTIONS

Include special instructions about care of vehicles, any hidden keys, and where registration papers are kept etc.

Donations to Make on My Behalf

NAME OF CHARITY	DONATION
Note: Large donations should be mentioned in your will	

38

Items of Value & Who Gets What

ITEM	GIVE THIS TO	CONTACT DETAILS
Note on blank page opposite any interesting history of these items.		

Items of Value & Who Gets What

ITEM	GIVE THIS TO	CONTACT DETAILS

Items of Value & Who Gets What

ITEM	GIVE THIS TO	CONTACT DETAILS

Clubs, Memberships and Organizations to Notify of My Death

ORGANIZATION	CONTACT NAME	PHONE OR EMAIL

Power, Gas, Phone, and Other Service Providers

COMPANY	ACCOUNT NUMBER	CONTACT DETAILS

Email and Social Media Details

COMPANY	USER NAME	PASSWORD

Facebook: Delete or Memorialize? (please circle one)

Other notes on Social Media:

After My Death

Organ donation?   YES   NO   (please circle one)

Conditions of donation:
_____

Blood type if known: _____

Burial or Cremation?   BURIAL   CREMATION   (please circle one)

OTHER
_____

Please bury me or spread ashes here:
_____

Type of Funeral?   RELIGIOUS   SECULAR   NO FUNERAL
(please circle one)

If religious please specify denomination:
_____

Hymns/Songs to play at my funeral

1.

2.

3.

Please Invite the Following People to My Funeral

NAME	CONTACT DETAILS

Please Invite the Following People to My Funeral

NAME	CONTACT DETAILS

Please Invite the Following People to My Funeral

NAME	CONTACT DETAILS

Final Letter to My Family

60

Special Instructions for My Service

62

Special Message to Mourners

64

Last Wishes

66

Words of Wisdom for My Friends and Family

68

Words of Wisdom for My Friends and Family

68

Additional Information for Friends and Family

Remember to keep this book up to date.

If you don't already have a will, you should get one soon.
Why not phone for an appointment with a lawyer now?

Having a will is the most important thing you can do
to help loved ones left behind. This book comes a close second.

www.ingramcontent.com/pod-product-compliance
Lightning Source LLC
Chambersburg PA
CBHW062227220526
45471CB00009B/3381